The Painter and the President

Gilbert Stuart's BRUSH with George Washington

SARAH ALBEE

ILLUSTRATED BY STACY INNERST

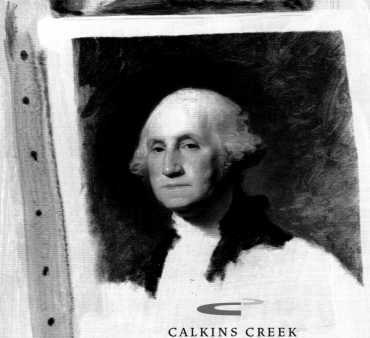

CALKINS CREEK

AN IMPRINT OF ASTRA BOOKS FOR YOUNG READERS

New York

"Now, sir, you must let me forget that you are General Washington and that I am Stuart, the painter."

"Mr. Stuart need never feel the need for forgetting who he is and who General Washington is."

Welcome to Philadelphia, 1796.
Want a picture of yourself?
You'll have to find an artist to paint your portrait.
(Photography hasn't been invented yet.)

And if you want to hire the best portrait painter in America?
Get Gilbert Stuart.

Here's his selfie.
(In the eighteenth century it's known as a self-portrait.)

George Washington is the president.
He's near the end of his second term.
He is sixty-four, worn down and weary.
He's looking forward to retirement.

George Washington *hates* sitting still
to have his portrait painted.

Gilbert Stuart is American, but he has just returned from living in England and Ireland, where he became famous for his portraits of lords and ladies, admirals and artists, diplomats and dignitaries.

George Washington is a man of action.
He'd rather sit on a horse than sit in a chair.

Most people love to pose for Gilbert Stuart.
There's no need to sit as still as a statue.
You can walk about the room.
You can chitchat with friends.
As he paints, Gilbert Stuart tells funny stories and cracks corny jokes.
The time simply flies.

After sitting for a portrait with Gilbert Stuart,
one person was asked if he was tired.

"Yes," the person replied. "With laughing."

For someone who hates sitting for portraits,
George Washington has posed for lots of portraits.

by Charles Peale Polk

by Robert Edge Pine

by John Trumbull

by Charles Willson Peale

by Charles Willson Peale

by Joseph Wright

He even sat for Gilbert Stuart once.
They did not hit it off.
(Can you tell?)

Other painters marvel at Gilbert Stuart's skill.
He paints quickly.
His faces seem lit from within.

How does he do it?

His dancing brush captures the very soul
of the person he is painting.

George Washington admits that portraits are important.
How else will future generations see him?
As he tells a friend, artists are "doorkeepers to the temple of fame."
George Washington understands the power of art.

Not everyone sees the charming side of Gilbert Stuart.
Sometimes the painter can be prickly.
If you say something insulting, he'll stop working.
He believes people should appreciate painters.
How else will future generations see you?
Gilbert Stuart understands the power of art.

Martha Washington convinces her husband
to pose for one more portrait.
It's for their grandchildren!
The president reluctantly agrees—
just so long as she doesn't hire
that infernal chatterbox Gilbert Stuart.

Martha hires Gilbert Stuart to paint the president's portrait.
(She'll have him paint *her* portrait, too.)

The painter is primed to paint the president!
If he can pull off a perfect portrait,
he can paint and sell copies of it (called *replicas*).

He'll be able to pay off all his debts.
(Gilbert Stuart tends to spend money faster than he can earn it.)

George Washington arrives at Gilbert Stuart's studio.
He wears a plain black suit and a pained expression.

The painter regards the president with horror.
What is wrong with George Washington's mouth?
The lower part of his face is puffy, and his lips are clenched
as though the man were playing an invisible trumpet.
George Washington's new false teeth don't fit well.

George Washington sits down.
His face assumes a gloomy expression
as he prepares to endure a tedious session.

The painter tries to put the president at ease
with lighthearted conversation.
But try as he might—and he tries *mightily*—
Gilbert Stuart cannot find a topic that interests the president.

Gilbert Stuart begins to paint.

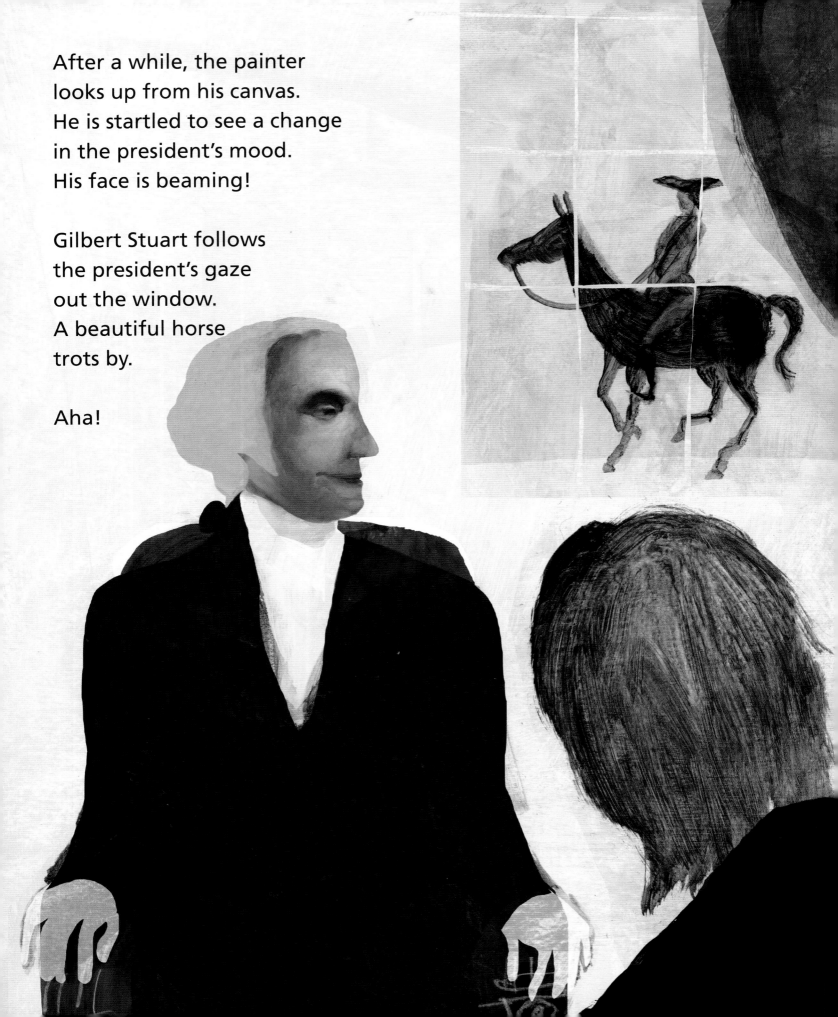

After a while, the painter
looks up from his canvas.
He is startled to see a change
in the president's mood.
His face is beaming!

Gilbert Stuart follows
the president's gaze
out the window.
A beautiful horse
trots by.

Aha!

Gilbert Stuart turns the topic to horse racing.
That works!
At last Gilbert Stuart has hit on a way to
light up the president's face.
The painter's brush dances around the canvas.

For their next appointment, the painter encourages
the president to bring along friends and family.
That works, too.
He's gone from glum to glad.

Gilbert Stuart also figures out
how to bring out the haughty,
commanding side of the
president's personality.
All the painter has to do is to show up late.

Gilbert Stuart finishes painting
the president's head.
The painter is pleased.
So pleased, in fact, that he leaves
the rest of the painting unfinished.
(He also leaves Martha's portrait unfinished.)

Over the next few years, Gilbert Stuart paints dozens
of replicas of the president's painting.
Many people buy them.
Money rolls in.

Gilbert Stuart never does finish that painting.
Even Martha Washington—
to her annoyance—
has to make do with a replica.

Whatever George Washington
thinks of Gilbert Stuart,
the president seems pleased
with the portrait.

This image just may be the
way future generations will
remember him.

George Washington was right.
Two and a half centuries later,
Gilbert Stuart's image of George Washington lives on.

The Go-To Painter for Presidential Portraits

Gilbert Stuart would eventually paint the portraits of six presidents.

John Adams

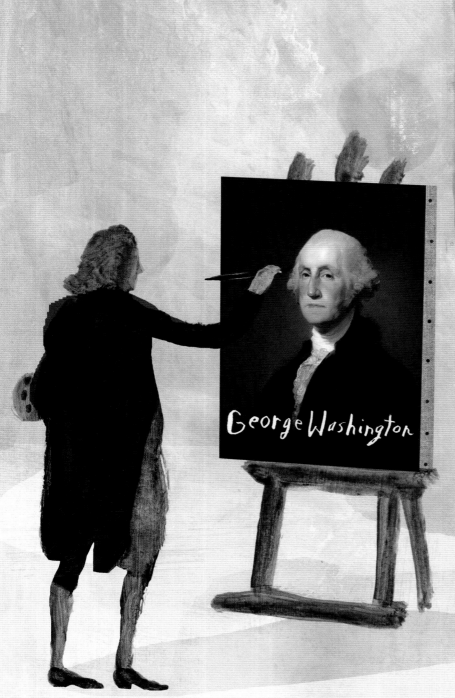

George Washington

The second president, John Adams, found Gilbert Stuart charming. "I should like to sit to Stuart from the first of January to the last of December, for he lets me do just as I please and keeps me constantly amused by his conversation."

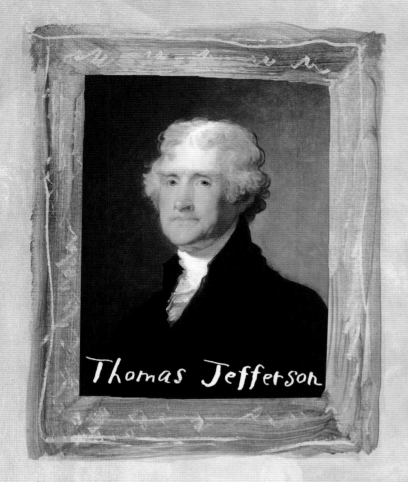

Thomas Jefferson

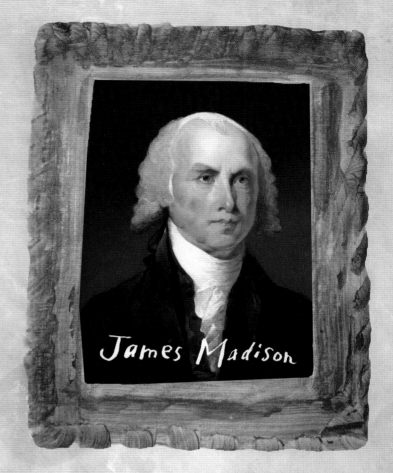

James Madison

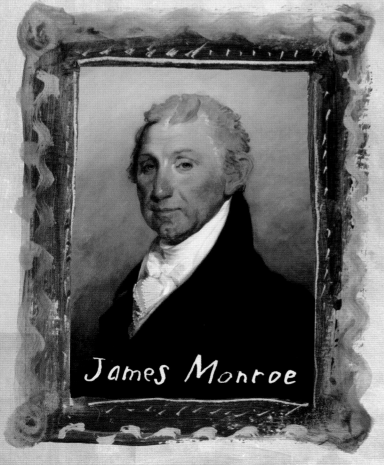

James Monroe

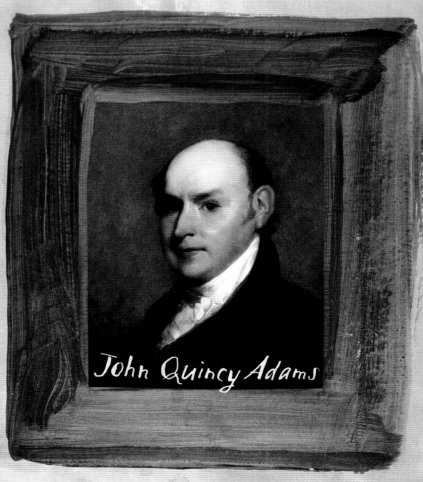

John Quincy Adams

1732: George Washington is born in the colony of Virginia.

1755: Gilbert Stuart is born in the colony of Rhode Island.

1759: George Washington marries Martha Custis, a widow with 2 children.

1761: The 7-year-old Gilbert Stuart has already begun to show real artistic talent. He moves with his family to nearby Newport, Rhode Island.

1769: The teenage Gilbert Stuart studies with the Scottish portrait painter Cosmo Alexander.

1771: Gilbert Stuart, working as Alexander's apprentice, travels with him to Scotland.

1772: Cosmo Alexander dies in Scotland, and Gilbert Stuart finds himself in serious financial trouble. He returns to Rhode Island to continue painting portraits.

1775: The American Revolution begins, and George Washington becomes commander in chief of the American army, fighting against the British.

———: Although Gilbert Stuart supports the American side in the war, he sets off for England to continue his painting career. He struggles financially, living mostly on crackers, but then becomes an assistant to the American painter Benjamin West. In London, Stuart begins to make a name for himself as a portrait painter.

1781: The British surrender to the Americans at Yorktown, Virginia, bringing an end to the Revolutionary War.

1783: George Washington retires from the army and returns to his plantation in Virginia.

1786: Still in London, Gilbert Stuart marries Charlotte Coates. They will eventually have 12 children—5 sons and 7 daughters. However, 7 of the 12 children will die young. The youngest, Jane, will grow up to be a painter.

1787: Gilbert Stuart accepts payment for many assignments but often fails to finish paintings. He also spends money freely. To escape his mounting debts, he and his family flee to Ireland. They live there for 6 years.

1789: Gilbert Stuart continues to paint many portraits, but he enjoys expensive wine and fine clothes. He is imprisoned in Ireland, probably because he fails to pay his debts.

———: George Washington is sworn in as the first president of the United States.

1790: Philadelphia becomes the temporary capital of the United States.

1792: George Washington is chosen for a second term as president.

1793: Gilbert Stuart and his growing family return to the US and settle briefly in New York. His goal is to paint the president, and after painting some brilliant portraits of rich and influential people, he receives a letter of introduction to George Washington.

1795: Gilbert Stuart moves to Philadelphia, where (in March) he paints the first portrait of George Washington.

1796: Gilbert Stuart begins a second portrait of George Washington, as well as one of Martha Washington. He never finishes either portrait but will paint at least 75 replicas of his painting of George Washington.

1797: George Washington retires from politics after declining a third term as president and returns to his home in Virginia.

1799: George Washington dies at age 67 of a throat infection.

1805: Gilbert Stuart moves to Boston, where he will live until his death. His financial troubles and neglect of his family continue for the rest of his life.

1814: As British soldiers set fire to the White House in the War of 1812, First Lady Dolley Madison and an enslaved man named Paul Jennings rescue a Gilbert Stuart portrait of George Washington.

1828: Suffering from a number of ailments, Stuart dies at the age of 72. His wife and surviving daughters cannot afford a gravestone, and he is buried in the Boston Commons in an unmarked grave.

George Washington's Tooth Troubles

In the eighteenth century, about the only way you could cure a toothache was to pull out the sore tooth. Over the years, dentists pulled out all of George Washington's real teeth, one by one. The springs and wires of his clumsy dentures rubbed his gums raw. Public speaking was difficult and painful. Eating was even worse. Because he had trouble chewing, George Washington could eat only soft, mushy food.

Why Is the Picture on the Dollar Bill Reversed?

To make an engraving, an engraver draws a careful copy of the painting. Then the drawing is laid down over a copper plate, and traced with a sharp metal engraver's tool, which cuts into the copper. After the plate is inked, a piece of paper is placed on top. Finally, the paper runs through a press, so that the image appears on the paper, but in reverse.

Picture Credits

Selected Bibliography

Barratt, Carrie Rebora, and Ellen G. Miles. *Gilbert Stuart*. New York: Metropolitan Museum of Art, 2004.

Chernow, Ron. *Washington: A Life*. New York: Penguin Books, 2010.

DeLorme, Eleanor Pearson. "Gilbert Stuart: Portrait of an Artist." *Winterthur Portfolio* 14, no. 4 (1979): 339–60.

Dunlap, William. *A History of the Rise and Progress of the Arts of Design in the United States*, ed. Frank W. Bayley and Charles E. Goodspeed, 3 vols. New and enlarged ed., Boston: C. E. Goodspeed, 1918.

Evans, Dorinda. *The Genius of Gilbert Stuart*. Princeton: Princeton University Press, 1999.

Fielding, Mantle. *Gilbert Stuart's Portraits of Washington*. Philadelphia: Wickersham Printing Co., 1923.

Flexner, James Thomas. *America's Old Masters*. New York: Doubleday & Co., 1980.

———. *Gilbert Stuart: A Great Life in Brief*. New York: Alfred A. Knopf, 1955.

Letter from George Washington to Lafayette, 28 May 1788, Founders Online, National Archives and Records Administration. Original source: *The Papers of George Washington*, Presidential Series, vol. 10, 1 March 1792–15 August 1792, ed. Robert F. Haggard and Mark A. Mastromarino. Charlottesville: University of Virginia Press, 2002: 515–516.

McLanathan, Richard. *Gilbert Stuart*. New York: Abrams, 1986.

Mason, George C. *The Life and Works of Gilbert Stuart*. New York: Charles Scribner's Sons, 1879.

Mayer, Lance, and Gay Myers. *American Painters on Technique: The Colonial Period to 1860*. Los Angeles: Getty Publications, 2011.

Morgan, John Hill, and Matthew Harris Jouett. *Gilbert Stuart and His Pupils: Together with the Complete Notes on Painting by Matthew Harris Jouett from Conversations with Gilbert Stuart in 1816*. New York: New-York Historical Society, 1939.

Oliver, Andrew. *Portraits of John Quincy Adams and His Wife*. Series IV: Adams Family Portraits of the Adams Papers Collection. Cambridge: Harvard University Press, 1970.

Rather, Susan. "Contrary Stuart." *American Art* 24, no. 1 (2010): 66–93.

Staiti, Paul J. "Gilbert Stuart's Washington." In *Of Arms and Artists: The American Revolution through Painters' Eyes*. New York: Bloomsbury, 2016.

Stuart, Jane. "The Stuart Portraits of Washington." *Scribner's Monthly* 12 (July 1876): 367–74.

———. "The Youth of Gilbert Stuart." *Scribner's Monthly* 13 (1877): 640–46.

———. "Anecdotes of Gilbert Stuart." *Scribner's Monthly* 14 (1877): 376–82.

Source Notes

The source of each quotation in this book is found below. Full source information is listed in the bibliography.

"Now, sir . . .": Chernow, *Washington: A Life*.

"Mr. Stuart need . . .": same as above.

"Yes . . .": Mayer and Myers, *American Painters on Technique: The Colonial Period to 1860*.

"doorkeepers to the . . .": letter from George Washington to Lafayette, 28 May 1788, Founders Online, National Archives and Records Administration.

"I should like . . .": Oliver, *Portraits of John Quincy Adams and His Wife*.

To Jon, as ever —*SA*

For three masterpieces:
Stuart, Olivia, and Jake —*SI*

Acknowledgments

Special thanks to Mary V. Thompson, research
historian, George Washington's Mount
Vernon, and to Ellen Miles.

Text copyright © 2024 by Sarah Albee
Illustrations copyright © 2024 by Stacy Innerst
All rights reserved. Copying or digitizing this book
for storage, display, or distribution in any other
medium is strictly prohibited.

For information about permission to reproduce
selections form this book, please contact
permissions@astrapublishinghouse.com.

Calkins Creek
An imprint of Astra Books for Young Readers,
a division of Astra Publishing House
astrapublishinghouse.com
Printed in China

ISBN: 978-1-6626-8000-7 (hc)
ISBN: 978-1-6626-8001-4 (eBook)
Library of Congress Control Number: 2023917979

First edition
10 9 8 7 6 5 4 3 2 1

Design by Barbara Grzeslo
The text is set in Frutiger LT Std.
The illustrations are done in acrylic, pencil,
and digital.